The City Dog *And The* Country Dog

Kent Satterlee III

The City Dog And The Country Dog

A Story About The Quest For Freedom

ARPress
ILLUMINATING IDEAS.
EMPOWERING VOICES

ARPress
45 Dan Road Suite 5
Canton MA 02021

Hotline: 1(888) 821-0229
Fax: 1(508) 545-7580

Ordering Information:
Quantity sales. Special discounts are available on quantity purchases by corporations, associations, and others. For details, contact the publisher at the address above.

Printed in the United States of America.

ISBN-13:	Softcover	979-8-89356-236-1
	eBook	979-8-89356-237-8

Library of Congress Control Number: 2024910592

Dedication

This book is dedicated to the beautiful property in the country, and its Owner, where many people come to get refreshed. It was inspired by Boone, a rescue Australian blue heeler, who found freedom in the country and showed his owner how to find freedom.

I also dedicate this book to my cousin, George W. Beeler Jr., DVM, who lost his earthly fight with cancer but gained eternal life in the process. His love for animals and people will never be forgotten.

"Lord, you alone are my inheritance, my cup of blessing. You guard all that is mine. The land you have given me is a pleasant land. What a wonderful inheritance!" Psalms 16:5-6 NLT

Credits

Sean of *The Good Dog*, who trained Boone and gave him a second chance at life.

Julia of *Northlake Veterinary Hospital*, whose love for Boone made him want to be a better dog. She never gave up on him.

Table of Contents

Introduction

The dog was rescued from an abusive situation and loved his new home but did not understand how to live within the boundaries set for him. He somehow felt it was okay to bite people, even his new master. The dog learned from his new master that obedience was hard for the moment but was a much better way to live. The dog's new master learned from the dog about companionship and the joy of being in the presence of his Master. They both learned that true freedom comes from knowing they can trust their masters.

Chapter One
The Adoption

The man and his son watched as the animal rescuers displayed the dogs in the field next to the cafe. The son had mentioned that he would like to have a dog to bring back to school with him. There was one dog in particular that caught his eye. It had a bluish fur and was especially playful with its handler.

The son stood and walked over to the field to see the dog more closely. He began to play with the dog and asked the handler if he could walk it. There seemed to be an instant connection between the son and the dog. The man walked over to the field to see the dog. He recognized the color and markings on the dog as an Australian blue heeler like the ones he grew up with on a ranch in east Texas.

The man spent his summers on the ranch helping his cousin bale hay and tend the cattle. The blue heelers herded the cows and forced them to go where the rancher wanted. They were quick and would bite the heels of the cows when they went their own way. Sadly, the man lost his cousin to cancer the year before. Seeing his son with the blue heeler reminded him of his cousin and the good times working on the ranch. The man missed his cousin very much, and the blue heeler made it seem as though his cousin was nearby.

The son asked his father if he could adopt the blue heeler. The man knew how much his son wanted a dog and had also felt the instant connection with this one. He gave his permission after consulting with his wife, and the son adopted the blue heeler that day. The son named the dog Boone, and they brought him home before the son went back to school.

Chapter Two
The Training Begins

When they got back to school, the son made a place for Boone to live. He had a fenced back yard, but Boone was able to jump the fence. He did not like being fenced in. The son would find Boone and bring him back. He tried to keep Boone inside the house, but Boone was not house-trained. He also liked to dig in the trash. Boone was very affectionate but did not understand boundaries and would jump up on people and scare them.

The son called his parents about Boone. They said that obedience training was the only way for Boone to adapt to his new life and not be a constant burden. They found a place nearby that would take Boone and teach him to obey; so the man and his son drove Boone over to his new temporary home to be trained. The trainer went to work and said Boone was responding well but that more time was needed. She said that Boone was strong willed and was easily distracted.

When the training was completed, the son picked up Boone and brought him back to school with a new set of commands for Boone to follow. Boone had been trained to "place" when commanded, in which he must remain until released. He was taught several other commands which the son began to reinforce. Boone seemed to be doing better but did not do well when the son left to attend classes. When Boone was released from his kennel, he became anxious and overly protective and began to bite other people that came to the house. This was unacceptable, so the son called his parents to come pick up Boone.

Chapter Three
The Bite

The man was very confused as to why Boone would begin biting people soon after completing obedience training. The training was comprehensive and had good results on other dogs. The trainer used food or "treats" to teach Boone how to obey. This technique worked well with most dogs, but Boone was able to pass the tests and get the treats but never really learned to obey. He obeyed to get the treat but then went back to doing whatever he wanted. The biting continued to be a problem. Boone bit a stranger walking through a hotel courtyard. He was on a leash but for some reason charged the man and bit his arm, tearing his shirt and drawing blood. The stranger was very upset and quickly got in his car and drove away. The stranger happened to be a well-known figure in the region and probably did not want the attention.

The man and his wife and son talked about what happened and tried to understand why Boone would do such a thing. They were quite concerned and began to research what might be the cause of this aberrant behavior. Was Boone just an aggressive dog that could not be trusted? Was he just trying to protect his owner? What was it? They called the animal shelter where Boone was adopted to see if he had exhibited any of these behaviors. The shelter was not aware of any aggressive behaviors; however, Boone had been rescued from a place that had several dogs caged up and exposed to the elements. The dogs were removed by the animal protective services. The previous owner of the dogs later came to claim the dogs and commit to taking better care of them but did not want Boone. He said Boone continually dug out of his pen and ran away.

If we fast forward, the man came to understand that Boone suffered from a form of anxiety. He became very anxious especially when it rained and thundered. He became anxious around other people he did not know, especially if he thought they threatened his master. Boone spent his formative years in a dog pen, exposed to the elements and without human affection. He was not taught proper behaviors or how to please his master. He had to fight for his share of the food. In short, he never had a home or a master that loved him and took care of him. He never learned obedience. He continually tried to escape from that miserable place.

The man and his wife tried to teach Boone to obey. He seemed to be responding but would dishonor his masters by disobeying their commands and misbehaving. One day before going to work, the man disciplined Boone with a stern "no" and a tap on the nose. Before the man knew what happened, Boone had bit down full force on his upper arm. The man was in pain and was greatly saddened that Boone would harm him in this way. He sat down in disappointment and wondered how this could happen. How could this dog attack his master after all the love and care his master had given!

After a few days had passed and the pain from the bite had subsided, the man felt there was only one thing he could do. He discussed it with his wife and son and decided to take Boone to the veterinarian to be euthanized. It was with much sadness that the man signed the paper to have Boone put down. When he returned home, his wife asked where he had been. When he explained that he had brought Boone to be euthanized, the man's wife began to cry and immediately called the veterinarian to stop the procedure. She wasn't able to accept this failure and putting Boone down.

After much searching, she found a dog trainer that specialized in hard cases. Boone responded well to the training. It seemed that he had always wanted to obey but needed the right structure and reinforcements. He needed to know that obedience was better than disobedience and that there were many benefits for obeying. He learned that it was much better to submit to his master. He found that there was security in trusting his master. He could count on being fed and having a place to sleep. He didn't have to worry about his needs being met.

Chapter Four
New Life

Boone came home with the man and his wife following his week of training. He was a different dog; he was attentive to his masters. He seemed to take pride in obeying their commands. The training was expensive, but it was what Boone needed to overcome his past. He still suffered with anxiety, but he found stability and confidence in his new life of obedience. He learned that they wanted nothing but good for him - that he would never again be hungry or cold at night. He would always have a good place to live and a warm bed to sleep.

The man would take Boone for walks around the neighborhood. Boone obeyed his commands flawlessly. Still, the man could not completely trust Boone because Boone had bit him and others. Boone still needed safe boundaries. One boundary was a muzzle that Boone wore when he was around other people. Boone seemed to understand that this was necessary and accepted the muzzle with no resistance.

One day, the man purchased a beautiful piece of property in the country. Boone loved to get in the truck and ride out to the property. There was a pond on the property that Boone could swim in, and there was lots of space to run. The man would get on the tractor and ride around the property to inspect and maintain it. Boone would follow without tiring. The property was not completely fenced, so Boone could run off if he wanted, but he never did. He enjoyed following the man around. He even protected the man when others came close; but, of course, this was not necessary. In time, Boone would learn this too.

When his master was working near one of the fence lines, Boone would pace back and forth along the fence. It was like a soldier protecting the base. This was probably a symptom of his anxiety, but he seemed to always position himself between the man and others. He was most happy when he could be near his master and obey his commands. He also loved to work, whether it be walking on a leash or fetching a ball or stick. He never tired of working as long as his master was leading him.

The man greatly enjoyed Boone's companionship. Each night when the man would go to bed, Boone somehow knew it was bedtime and would follow the man to the bedroom and get on his pad next to the man's bed. He would remain there until it was time to wake up and the man would get up and make the coffee. At times when it rained and thundered, Boone would become anxious and place his paws up on the bed to get assurance that things were alright. Boone may have remembered the times when he lived in that dog pen and it rained and thundered. There was no one there to comfort him and tell him it was okay.

Wherever the man went, Boone would follow. At times when the man had to leave without Boone, he assured Boone that he was coming back. Boone would stand by the door and watch the man pack up and drive off. When the man returned, Boone would wag his tail intensely and wait for the man to give him a hug. He made a kind of whistling sound when the man hugged him which seemed to express his happiness that the man was home.

As time went on, Boone became more attentive to the man's voice. The man could speak very softly and Boone would obey. Boone was still a dog and wanted to do what dogs love to do like chase squirrels and dig holes, but he was changing from a self-focus to a man-focus. It seemed that Boone had a desire to always be listening for the man to speak a command or go to work. This came as Boone had all of his needs met, and he did not have to worry about his next meal or whether he would be cold at night. He still made mistakes and failed to obey at times, but it was clear that his attitude had changed. He found that submission was good, and it brought many benefits like words of affirmation and pats on the head. It seemed that Boone now saw his adoption as complete. He would not ever have to go back to the cruel master. His new master would always love him and take care of him.

Chapter Five
The Man and his New Master

The man loved Boone very much. Boone would remind the man of spending time on the ranch with his cousin as a boy. These were happy memories which the man held onto throughout his life, especially during hard times and times where he himself experienced much anxiety. As a young man, he experienced the same stresses and difficulties as other men but was overcome by anxiety. This caused him to feel like things were not going to work out. When the man remembered the love and companionship he received from his cousin on the ranch, it helped the anxiety be more tolerable.

Before the man came to know his new Master, he had a cruel master who constantly lied to him. The cruel master told the man that he would never measure up. The cruel master allowed the man to do whatever he wanted and even tempted him to do unhealthy things. The man didn't have a strong foundation to resist the temptations, and so he did things that hurt himself and others. The man thought about how Boone would dig out of the dog pen when he was with his cruel master and how he must have hurt himself and others. Boone was probably trying to get his needs met - like hunger and need for companionship. Like Boone, the man was probably trying to get his needs met, but neither one found what they were longing for until they found their new masters and learned to trust them to provide for their needs.

The man learned about the benefits of trusting his Master by watching how Boone learned to trust his new master. Boone never had to worry about getting his needs met with his new master, but at first, he didn't understand that. All he knew was how the cruel master treated him. He always worried whether he was going to get fed and whether he would have to sleep in the cold. His new master provided for everything Boone would ever need but until Boone submitted to the new master's care, he could not fully trust that his new master was good and wanted the best for him. As the man observed this progression in Boone, he thought of his own relationship with his Master. He realized that he still worried about whether his needs would be met and would become anxious at times when things looked bad or were not going as planned.

It was not easy for Boone to submit to his new master. He had learned to fend for himself and fight for what he wanted. He didn't care who he hurt in the process. Sometimes when the man played a little rough with Boone, Boone would snap at the man. Boone needed to learn to respect his new master at all times, not just when his master was doing something he liked or wanted. In time, Boone learned that the man loved him and would never hurt him.

The man thought about the times he disregarded his Master because he was too busy or when life seemed to get tough. He would even get angry with his Master when he didn't get what he wanted. The man would sometimes take matters into his own hands instead of trusting his Master to show him the best way. It was hard for the man to wait for his Master to provide for his needs. He would get frightened and anxious. As the man learned to submit to his Master and to honor him, he saw that everything he needed was made available in just the right time. The man also saw that his Master wanted to give him more than he could even imagine, but the man needed to learn to take care of the things he already had before he could take care of more. The man began to realize that there were no limitations to what his Master could do.

The man retired from his job and spent more time on the property in the country with Boone. Boone became very attuned to the man's voice and loved to come put his paws up on the man's lap and listen to the man talk to him. The man would rub Boone's head and tell him he was a good dog. When Boone would run around on the property chasing squirrels or swimming in the pond, the man had a certain sound he would make, and Boone would come running back.

Since the man did not have to go to the office every day, he would wake up and sit with some coffee and read a story that his Master had written. The story was very long, and it had many twists and turns; but each day as the man read, he learned more about his Master. He learned that his Master was kind and merciful and slow to anger, but he learned also that his Master was jealous and especially did not like his people to get fooled by the cruel masters. He loved his people too much to see them fall for the tricks of the cruel masters. They would fool the people into thinking their ways were better, but in the end, they lead to destruction.

The man came to know his Master more intimately and knew he could trust him. He gladly began to submit to the commands of his Master. In the Master's Story, the man read about many wonderful plans the Master had and that he was invited to cooperate in those plans. It was really hard for the man to believe all that, but the more he listened, the more he believed it was true.

Chapter Six
Freedom

Boone's obedience training was a long journey, and it's not complete; but it's not all Boone's fault. Yes, Boone was a difficult case, but he had many scars from his cruel master. Those scars made it hard for him to trust his new master.

Similarly, the man's obedience training was a long journey, and it's also not complete. And like Boone, the man had many scars from his cruel master. As the man read the Master's Story, he learned that his scars would heal over time as he learned to trust his new Master. The things the cruel master said to the man, like "you won't ever measure up" would no longer be remembered. The words written in the Master's Story would replace them and would become his new identity. The old things passed away, and all things became new. The cruel master told the man it was doubtful that he could ever love someone enough to get married. But the man learned from his new Master that eternal love now lived inside of him, and he could have that kind of love. Because of the intimidation from the cruel master, the man would sometimes get shaken when spoken down to by a bigger or more important man. However, the man learned from his new Master that he was a mighty warrior, and there was no man too big or too important. The Master's Story had everything the man needed, and best of all it taught him to obey his Master. At first it seemed that obedience training was hard and painful, but once the man began to understand how his Master loved him and cared for him, he would simply submit. It was really quite easy that way.

The man realized that his new Master had many adventures in store for him - adventures like he read in the Master's Story. The adventures seemed impossible from a human perspective, but the Master would give strength to his people and enable them to overcome big obstacles. The Master always had a much bigger plan than the people in the Story could see at the time. There were ups and downs. They would sometimes lose faith in the Master and go back to their old ways. This too was part of the obedience training - to obey even when things didn't make any sense. It became easy to obey the Master when the man felt him nearby, but there were times when he felt that the Master was far away, and things looked like they were falling apart. At times like this, the man knew he needed to hear from his Master - he needed reassurance. He would read the Master's Story to find out what the people in the Story would do in times like this. The man came to realize that his Master would speak to him through the Story.

One of the adventures that his Master had prepared for the man was the beautiful piece of property in the country. The property had been cultivated for many years by an older gentleman, now 90 years old. The older gentleman could feel God's presence on the land and worked hard to improve the land. When the man and his wife discovered the land, it became clear that the older gentleman had cooperated with God to make the land even more beautiful and prosperous. He had planted the now majestic oak trees and flowering bushes, and he had built a beautiful pond and filled it with fish. The older gentleman was very proud of his work and wanted the land to continue to prosper and be a blessing to others. The man and his wife loved the land and could instantly see God's hand in making the land so prosperous. The man knew he needed to go to his Master and see if his Master wanted him to buy the land. The man knew that his Master would have to accomplish this because the man could not afford to buy the land. The man again went to the Master's Story and read about what the Master had done before for his people. He could see that indeed his Master wanted him to take possession of the land, and the Master would provide all he needed.

The man was overwhelmed by his Master's generosity and faith in him to care for the land. The man realized there would be difficult challenges that must be overcome in securing the land, and he needed to continue to obey what his Master was saying. He knew there was always the risk that he would lose the land if his Master did not provide. The man and his wife believed their Master had plans for the land and wanted to be sure to obey what their Master was doing. They wanted to honor their Master, and so they deeded the land to Him. They wanted Him to be the owner, and they the caretakers.

As the man grew older, he began to realize that his Master would never leave him; although at times he felt that his Master was far away. He realized that his Master was training him to trust in what he had already learned about his Master's character. There was a degree of trust that would grow stronger as the man had to think about how to respond in these difficult times and whether he really believed what his Master had said. Would he run away like Boone had done with his cruel master or get angry with someone in the same way that Boone would bite? Would he go back to listening to the lies of the cruel master? Those lies always made the man feel worse. Little by little, the man learned that the cruel master had nothing good for him and actually wanted to destroy him. And little by little, the man learned that trusting his new Master always had a good ending. Best of all, the man learned to distinguish the voice of his new Master from the voice of the cruel master and to listen intently when his Master spoke. It was in learning to listen to his Master and feeling his presence that the man found true freedom.

When Boone was with his cruel master, he lived in a cage. He became very skilled at escaping. He was a "city dog" and found his freedom by escaping from the fences that held him in bondage. When Boone went to live with his new master and the fences removed, he could run away if he wanted; but he didn't want to. He found great pleasure in being with his master. He was now a "country dog".

Chapter Seven
Work

Whenever Boone and the man would go to work, the man would notice that Boone would look intently into his eyes as if he were asking, "what should I do?". Boone would be waiting for a command or watching for any move that the man would make. The man recalled reading in the Master's Story times when men of ages past were faced with difficult problems, and they would ask the Master what to do. Those men believed that the Master would always show them what to do, and he did. Boone helped the man remember that if he paid close attention to his Master he would never have to fear indecision or face a problem alone.

Boone was always very excited about going to work. It's as if he was created for that purpose. The man wondered if humans were different than dogs in that respect - perhaps people didn't like to work, but it could be that people were just trying to do the wrong work. Instead of doing what they were made for, they would go do their own thing and not find much pleasure in it. By watching Boone, the man realized that work could be enjoyed if he was doing what his Master wanted.

Boone responded immediately whenever his master would say, "Boone come". He trusted that his master would always have something good for him, like a treat or a walk. The man learned that when his Master would say to him, "Come, follow me", He had something good for him, like a new adventure or maybe even some fun work to do. The man would sometimes ask, "Where are we going?", but they would always wind up in the right place.

The man enjoyed fishing in the pond on the property in the country. When the man would cast into the water, Boone would stand in the water and watch where the lure hit. He would watch closely as the man reeled it in. When the man would catch a fish, Boone would jump up to get it as if it belonged to him. Boone, no doubt, felt that he helped catch the fish. The man thought about how his Master was always working and wanted the man to participate in what he was doing. It was exciting when something big got accomplished, and the man felt he was a part of it; but he knew that he could not have done it by himself. The man remembered how he had discovered the beautiful property seemingly by accident, not at all knowing that his Master had been planning this. It seemed that his Master had been working at it for some time and was waiting for the man to come participate in what he was doing.

One day, the man heard Boone barking and growling ferociously. He looked out to see what was happening and saw that a large black snake had crawled under the fence into the backyard. Boone had corralled it and looked as if he was going to attack it, but the snake escaped. The man was thankful Boone saw that part of his job was to protect his home from intruders. The man appreciated Boone's loyalty and his desire to protect him. It helped him realize how his Master appreciated the man's loyalty. The Master was fully able to accomplish things without the man's help but desired the man's companionship and his willingness to join in on whatever he was doing.

In the Master's Story, there were many times when men of ages past accomplished amazing feats when they worked alongside the Master. One such story involved a man named Gideon. He was probably the most unlikely man that the Master could choose to work with him because he was not much of a man in his own eyes and his family had no particular pedigree. The Master instructed him to gather up some men to help him fight a terrible enemy but then told Gideon to send most of the men home. When the job was finished and the battle won, it was quite clear that the Master did most of the work, but Gideon became a hero in the land because he trusted the Master and gave the Master credit for the amazing victory. The Master knew he could trust Gideon to do even bigger jobs.

When Boone and the man would work together, the man thought about all the times in the Master's Story when the Master chose to work with some unlikely candidates. The man realized that the natural ability of those men and women was not very important to the Master; rather, it was their ability to not trust in themselves but to instead trust the Master. The Master always seemed to be most happy when this happened. It seemed that the Master loved to do all the hard work if people would trust him and not try to take over the job. This was very humbling, but it appeared this was the way the Master wanted to get things done.

Boone's genetic makeup called for him to be a herding dog - to "heel" cows and sheep - and to draw them in to wherever the rancher or shepherd wanted. It was easy to see these genetic characteristics in Boone even though there were no cows or sheep to herd on the property in the country. Boone's favorite thing to do besides follow his master around was to find unwanted rodents in the barn and around trees and bushes. He searched endlessly for anything that moved. He would dig and climb or do what was necessary to find them. He usually did not hurt the animals; he was just doing what he enjoyed and was made to do. All day long he would work at this.

One day as the man was working in the barn, there was quite a racket coming from the area of the barn where the tractors were kept. The man walked over to see what was happening. Boone had climbed up on the tractor and was hunting for something - no doubt looking for some rodent that had found a home in the engine compartment. This kept him busy for hours. There was nothing that could distract him from this job.

As the man watched this obsession, he was reminded of what Jesus told his disciples in the Master's Story. He said to go out into the world and share the Good News that Jesus came to earth to find and to save the lost. His desire was that all people would be saved and have eternal life. Jesus seemed to be most interested in finding the unwanted and the unloved. He spoke of finding the lost sheep that had wandered off from the fold and were in danger of being attacked by predators. These predators would rob, kill, and destroy. He was tireless in this pursuit, even when his disciples told him he should eat or rest. Jesus said he could not rest until his job was finished.

To this day, the followers of Jesus will not rest until the Good News is shared throughout the world and the lost are found. Jesus told them he would return soon and that he was preparing a wonderful place for them. The man thought about these words of Jesus often and wondered if this place that Jesus was preparing would be anything like the beautiful property in the country. He somehow knew this place could not be complete without Boone - he knew that Jesus was working to make it perfect in every way.

Epilogue

Boone still wears a muzzle when he is around other people, but he readily submits to his master. He still digs holes in the back yard, no doubt a habit he learned to find food while caged by his cruel master. The man still makes mistakes - he gets frustrated at times, he loses his patience, he gets angry, and he still gets anxious at times. His failures drive him to his Master, and he must ask for mercy once again. His Master assures him that his mercies are new each day and not to worry. His Master doesn't expect perfection, just the man's devotion. Everything else will follow.

His Master made sure of that by sending His Spirit to live inside him and to do what he could not do on his own. He also gave the man a prayer, "lead us not into temptation, but deliver us from the evil one." His Master was fully able to deliver and would take great pleasure in seeing his people set free.

The beautiful property in the country became a special place for the man and his family. He felt very close to his Master when he visited the property. Others who came to visit said they felt the same way. It became a place of rest and refreshment for many, and Boone had a place where he could run and swim to his heart's delight. Boone took great pleasure in working with his master and would follow close behind him. Like Boone, the man took great pleasure in being with his Master and in doing the work his Master was doing. They both knew they could run away if they wanted - there were no longer any fences to contain them, but they didn't want to. Like Boone, the man was now a "country dog".

Boone still follows his master around. He wants his master to always be in view. This seemed a little strange to the man's wife and other people who knew them, but the man always enjoyed Boone's companionship and appreciated Boone's loyalty. He thought about how his Master must enjoy the companionship and loyalty of his friends. He realized that Boone wanted his master to always be in view because that is where he felt secure, and indeed that is where the man felt most secure - when his Master was in view.

The man had many battles to overcome throughout his life. Boone's companionship was always a great help to him as he endured the battles. His biggest battle was for his own life as cancer threatened to take it. The doctors said there was no cure and that it would eventually spread to his bones. The man once again needed to hear from his Master about what to do. In the Master's Story, the Master said he sent his Son to earth to save us from sin and all its effects, including sickness and disease. The man decided to trust what his Master said. He became convinced that his Master was always working to make things better, indeed, perfect.

Excerpts from the Master's Story

"LORD, you alone are my inheritance, my cup of blessing. You guard all that is mine. The land you have given me is a pleasant land. What a wonderful inheritance!"
Psalms 16:5-6 NLT

"The righteous person faces many troubles, but the Lord comes to the rescue each time. For the Lord protects the bones of the righteous; not one of them is broken!"
Psalms 34:19-20 NLT

"I prayed to the Lord, and he answered me. He freed me from all my fears. Those who look to him for help will be radiant with joy; no shadow of shame will darken their faces."
Psalms 34:4-5 NLT

"God sent a man, John the Baptist, to tell about the light so that everyone might believe because of his testimony. John himself was not the light; he was simply a witness to tell about the light. The one who is the true light, who gives light to everyone, was coming into the world. He came into the very world he created, but the world didn't recognize him. He came to his own people, and even they rejected him. But to all who believed him and accepted him, he gave the right to become children of God. They are reborn—not with a physical birth resulting from human passion or plan, but a birth that comes from God. So the Word became human and made

his home among us. He was full of unfailing love and faithfulness. And we have seen his glory, the glory of the Father's one and only Son."
John 1:6-14 NLT

"For this is how God loved the world: He gave his one and only Son, so that everyone who believes in him will not perish but have eternal life. God sent his Son into the world not to judge the world, but to save the world through him."
John 3:16-17 NLT

"Jesus replied, "If you only knew the gift God has for you and who you are speaking to, you would ask me, and I would give you living water."
John 4:10 NLT

"The woman said, "I know the Messiah is coming—the one who is called Christ. When he comes, he will explain everything to us." Then Jesus told her, "I AM the Messiah!"
John 4:25-26 NLT

"Then Jesus explained: "My nourishment comes from doing the will of God, who sent me, and from finishing his work. You know the saying, 'Four months between planting and harvest.' But I say, wake up and look around. The fields are already ripe for harvest. The harvesters are paid good wages, and the fruit they harvest is people brought to eternal life. What joy awaits both the planter and the harvester alike! You know the saying, 'One plants and another harvests.' And it's true. I sent you to harvest where you didn't plant; others had already done the work, and now you will get to gather the harvest."
John 4:34-38 NLT

"But Jesus replied, "My Father is always working, and so am I."
John 5:17 NLT

"I tell you the truth, those who listen to my message and believe in God who sent me have eternal life. They will never be condemned for their sins, but they have already passed from death into life. "And I assure you that the time is coming, indeed it's here now, when the dead will hear my voice—the voice of the Son of God. And those who listen will live. The

Father has life in himself, and he has granted that same life-giving power to his Son."
John 5:24-26 NLT

"The Lord brought his people out of Egypt, loaded with silver and gold; and not one among the tribes of Israel even stumbled. Egypt was glad when they were gone, for they feared them greatly. The Lord spread a cloud above them as a covering and gave them a great fire to light the darkness. They asked for meat, and he sent them quail; he satisfied their hunger with manna—bread from heaven. He split open a rock, and water gushed out to form a river through the dry wasteland. For he remembered his sacred promise to his servant Abraham. So he brought his people out of Egypt with joy, his chosen ones with rejoicing. He gave his people the lands of pagan nations, and they harvested crops that others had planted. All this happened so they would follow his decrees and obey his instructions. Praise the Lord!"
Psalms 105:37-45 NLT

"Jesus told them, "This is the only work God wants from you: Believe in the one he has sent.""
John 6:29 NLT

"Simon Peter replied, "Lord, to whom would we go? You have the words that give eternal life. We believe, and we know you are the Holy One of God."
John 6:68-69 NLT

"Jesus spoke to the people once more and said, "I am the light of the world. If you follow me, you won't have to walk in darkness, because you will have the light that leads to life."
John 8:12 NLT

"So, if the Son sets you free, you are truly free."
John 8:36 NLT

"But the one who enters through the gate is the shepherd of the sheep. The gatekeeper opens the gate for him, and the sheep recognize his voice and come to him. He calls his own sheep by name and leads them out. After

he has gathered his own flock, he walks ahead of them, and they follow him because they know his voice. They won't follow a stranger; they will run from him because they don't know his voice."
John 10:2-5NLT

"Yes, I am the gate. Those who come in through me will be saved. They will come and go freely and will find good pastures. The thief's purpose is to steal and kill and destroy. My purpose is to give them a rich and satisfying life."
John 10:9=1- NLT

"I am the good shepherd; I know my own sheep, and they know me, just as my Father knows me and I know the Father. So I sacrifice my life for the sheep."
John 10:14-15 NLT

"Take delight in the Lord, and he will give you your heart's desires."
Psalms 37:4 NLT

"For the Lord is the Spirit, and wherever the Spirit of the Lord is, there is freedom."
2 Corinthians 3:17 NLT

"So now there is no condemnation for those who belong to Christ Jesus. And because you belong to him, the power of the life-giving Spirit has freed you from the power of sin that leads to death."
Romans 8:1-2 NLT

"After saying all these things, Jesus looked up to heaven and said, "Father, the hour has come. Glorify your Son so he can give glory back to you. For you have given him authority over everyone. He gives eternal life to each one you have given him. And this is the way to have eternal life—to know you, the only true God, and Jesus Christ, the one you sent to earth. I brought glory to you here on earth by completing the work you gave me to do. Now, Father, bring me into the glory we shared before the world began."
John 17:1-5 NLT

"I'm not asking you to take them out of the world, but to keep them safe from the evil one."
John 17:15 NLT

"And lead us not into temptation, but deliver us from the evil one."
Matthew 6:13 NIV

"Remember me, Lord, when you show favor to your people; come near and rescue me. Let me share in the prosperity of your chosen ones. Let me rejoice in the joy of your people; let me praise you with those who are your heritage."
Psalms 106:4-5 NLT

"Your word is a lamp to guide my feet and a light for my path."
Psalms 119:105NLT

"My life constantly hangs in the balance, but I will not stop obeying your instructions. The wicked have set their traps for me, but I will not turn from your commandments. Your laws are my treasure; they are my heart's delight. I am determined to keep your decrees to the very end."
Psalms 119:109-112 NLT

"I rejoice in your word like one who discovers a great treasure."
Psalms 119:162 NLT

"I long for your rescue, Lord, so I have obeyed your commands. I have wandered away like a lost sheep; come and find me, for I have not forgotten your commands."
Psalms 119:166, 176 NLT

"He sent out his word and healed them, snatching them from the door of death."
Psalms 107:20 NLT

"And then he told them, "Go into all the world and preach the Good News to everyone. Anyone who believes and is baptized will be saved. But anyone who refuses to believe will be condemned. These miraculous signs will accompany those who believe: They will cast out demons in my name,

and they will speak in new languages. They will be able to handle snakes with safety, and if they drink anything poisonous, it won't hurt them. They will be able to place their hands on the sick, and they will be healed." When the Lord Jesus had finished talking with them, he was taken up into heaven and sat down in the place of honor at God's right hand. And the disciples went everywhere and preached, and the Lord worked through them, confirming what they said by many miraculous signs."
Mark 16:15-20 NLT

Boone's Adoption

Boone on the Property in the Country

Boone Eyeing Fish He Just Helped Catch

Boone at Home in the Country